Maple Leaf

Janet Gurtler

Weigl

Published by Weigl Educational Publishers Limited
6325 10th Street SE
Calgary, Alberta T2H 2Z9
Website: www.weigl.com

Library and Archives Canada Cataloguing in Publication

Gurtler, Janet
          Maple leaf / Janet Gurtler.
(Canadian icons)
Includes index.
ISBN 978-1-77071-661-2 (bound).--ISBN 978-1-77071-667-4 (pbk.)
          1. Maple leaf (Emblem)--Juvenile literature.
I. Title. II. Series: Canadian icons

JC347.C3G88 2011   j929.90971   C2011-900806-8

Printed in the United States of America in North Mankato, Minnesota
1 2 3 4 5 6 7 8 9 0 15 14 13 12 11

052011
WEP37500

Editor: Heather Kissock
Art Director: Terry Paulhus

Weigl acknowledges Getty Images as the primary image supplier for this title.

We acknowledge the financial support of the Government of Canada through the Canada Book Fund for our
publishing activities.

CONTENTS

4   What is a Maple Leaf?

7   Canada's Maple Trees

8   An Early Symbol

10   A Song for Canada

12   A National Tree

14   The Maple Leaf Flag

16   Maple Leaf Money

18   On Guard for the Maple Leaf

20   Proud to be Canadian

22   Make a Maple Leaf Pin

23   Find Out More

24   Glossary/Index

What is a Maple Leaf?

Maple leaves grow on maple trees. They are the flat parts that grow from the tree branches. A maple leaf is wide and has several points.

The maple leaf is a **symbol** of Canada. It is placed on items to show they are from Canada.

Canada's Maple Trees

Canada is home to 10 different kinds of maple tree. Every province has at least one kind of maple tree growing in it. The best-known maple trees in Canada are the red maple tree and the sugar maple tree.

An Early Symbol

The maple tree and its leaves have been symbols of Canada for a long time. When Europeans first came to Canada, they saw **Aboriginal Peoples** using maple tree sap as sugar.

The Europeans began to use the sap in the same way. It became an important food source for them. They began to use the maple leaf as a symbol for their new home.

A Song for Canada

When Canada became a country in 1867, a man named Alexander Muir wrote a song to celebrate. The song was called "The Maple Leaf For Ever." In the song, the maple leaf stands for Canada. For many years, people called "The Maple Leaf For Ever" Canada's **national anthem**.

11

A National Tree

The maple tree and its leaves continued to be used as a symbol of Canada. Over time, people all over the world came to know that a red maple leaf stood for Canada. To show how important the maple tree was to Canada, the government made it Canada's **official** tree in 1996.

The Maple Leaf Flag

In 1965, Prime Minister Lester Pearson showed Canada's new flag for the first time. The flag had a picture of a red maple leaf in its centre. Some people call it the maple leaf flag because of this. The maple leaf flag now waves all over the world as a symbol of Canada.

Maple Leaf Money

In the past, the maple leaf appeared on all Canadian coins. Now, it is seen most often on the penny. The Canadian penny has two maple leaves on it.

The maple leaf can also be seen on special coins. The Royal Canadian **Mint** has made gold and silver coins that feature the maple leaf.

On Guard for the Maple Leaf

Canadian soldiers have used the maple leaf as their **emblem** since World War I. Maple leaf badges are sewn onto their uniforms. The maple leaf is sometimes painted on their equipment as well. The maple leaf tells people that the soldiers and their equipment are from Canada.

Proud to Be Canadian

Canadians use the maple leaf in many ways. When Canadians go to other countries, they often wear maple leaf pins on their clothes. The pins let others know the wearers are from Canada.

Every year on July 1, Canadians wish Canada a happy birthday. People paint the maple leaf on their face and wave maple leaf flags.

Make a Maple Leaf Pin

Supplies

scissors

pin

glue

acrylic sealer
spray

red construction
paper

1. For each pin, cut out ten maple leaf shapes from the paper.

2. Glue all of the leaves on top of each other. Line the edges up as evenly as possible so that the leaves are stacked. Let the glue dry.

3. When the glue is dry, spray the stack with a few coats of acrylic sealer. Let it dry between coats.

4. When the final coat of sealer is dry, glue the pin on to the back of the stack.

5. Wear your pin to show people you are Canadian.

Find Out More

To learn more about Canada's maple leaf, visit these websites.

Canadian Heritage—The Maple Leaf
www.pch.gc.ca/pgm/ceem-cced/
symbl/o3-eng.cfm

eHow—Why is the Maple Leaf a Canadian Symbol?
www.ehow.com/about_5082618_
maple-leaf-canadian-symbol.html

**Canadiana Connection—
The Maple Leaf**
www.canadianaconnection.com/
cca/mapleleaf.htm

Glossary

Aboriginal Peoples: the first peoples to live in Canada

emblem: a sign or figure that stands for something

mint: a place where coins are made

national anthem: a country's official song

official: approved for use

symbol: something used to represent something else

Index

flag 14, 20

Maple Leaf For Ever, The 10

maple tree 4, 7, 8, 12

penny 16

sap 8